DK READERS

MARVEL
THE AVENGERS

AVENGERS ASSEMBLE!

Written by Victoria Taylor

The origins

When the mighty Avengers assemble, Super Villains had better watch out! Earth's premier team of Super Heroes is not afraid to tackle even the most fearsome villains.

The team was formed when Loki, the God of Mischief, tried to lure his brother Thor into battle. Loki tricked the Hulk into destroying a railroad knowing that Thor would stop him.

The Hulk's sidekick Rick Jones tried to call for some help from the Fantastic Four, another team of Super Heroes.

Revenge
Loki wanted revenge for being imprisoned on the Isle of Silence for crimes against Thor.

However, his message reached
Thor along with Ant-Man, the
Wasp and Iron Man instead.
They worked out Loki's plan and
joined forces to defeat him.

The team was so successful that
Ant-Man suggested that they should
stay together to fight the foes that no
Super Hero could fight alone.

Birth of a team

A new Super Hero team had been formed, but it needed a super name! The Wasp suggested "The Avengers" and everyone agreed. The first recruits were Hawkeye, Scarlet Witch and Quicksilver. The Hulk's behaviour was too unpredictable so he left the team. He was replaced by Captain America, who is more reliable than the Hulk. Cap also became the leader of the group and under his leadership the Avengers became much stronger. Over the years, many brave heroes have been proud to call themselves Avengers. Come and meet some of the Super Heroes who have answered the call "Avengers Assemble!"

Ant-Man

Scientist Henry "Hank" Pym
discovered particles that can help
people change in size. He named them
Pym Particles and uses them to shrink
himself down to the size of an ant.
Now known as Ant-Man, Pym is
one of the founding members of the
Avengers and uses his scientific skills
to create useful weapons for the team.

Giant-Man
After becoming
jealous of his
larger team-
mates, Pym
used the
particles to
increase his
size and took
on the identity
of Giant-Man.

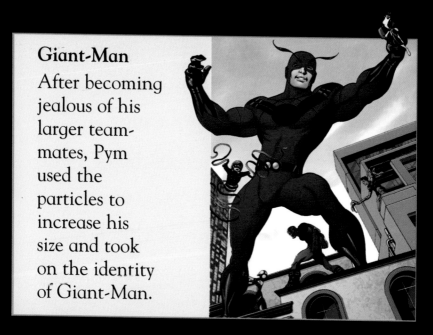

Ant-Man also has a cybernetic helmet that allows him to control ants. Using the helmet, he can communicate with them, hitch a ride on the back of flying ants and summon a whole colony of ants whenever he needs it.

The Wasp

The Wasp changes her costume
as often as the Hulk gets in a rage.
She can shrink to the size of an insect,
grow wings and
fire a powerful
sting that can
stop enemies in
their tracks.

She can also communicate
with all forms of
insect life.

The Wasp
was once a
wealthy woman
named Janet van
Dyne. She asked
Ant-Man to
help her become a

*The Wasp eventually married
her fellow Avenger, Ant-Man.
It created quite a buzz in the team!*

Super Hero in order to avenge
her father's murder. Ant-Man gave
her Pym Particles, which gave her
the ability to shrink or grow in size.
He also implanted cells into her
shoulders that helped her to
grow wings and fly
when she shrank
in size.

The Incredible Hulk

When scientist Bruce Banner was accidentally struck by gamma rays he was turned into a Super Hero – the Hulk. Now, every time he feels angry or scared, his muscles bulge and burst out of his clothes and he grows to a gigantic size. He also turns green! The angrier he gets, the stronger he becomes. However, the Hulk is very unpredictable and uncontrollable. He is not always a good team player, so the Hulk is not a permanent member of the Avengers.

Bruce Banner was recruited by the U.S. Army to develop weapons while still in high school.

The Mighty Thor

Thor is the Norse God of Thunder and Lightning. He was sent down to Earth from his home in Asgard by his father, Odin, in order to learn humility.

On Earth, Thor lived as an ordinary human named Dr. Donald Blake. Years later, a message from Odin led Dr. Blake to a walking cane. When he struck the ground with it, the cane changed into Mjolnir, a magical hammer. Thor had first received Mjolnir as a child and was pleased to be reunited with his mighty hammer. Dr. Blake was ready to become Thor again.

With the unbreakable Mjolnir, Thor can strike the ground and produce lightning to attack his foes.

Captain America

Captain America's costume and shield are decorated with stars and stripes, just like the U.S. flag. A symbol of American patriotism, he is always ready to defend citizens in danger. Cap used to be a skinny guy named Steve Rogers until a government experiment turned him into a Super Hero. He was given Super Soldier Serum, which increased his size, strength and stamina. He joined the Avengers when the team freed him from a block of ice.

Super shield

Captain America's shield can be thrown at enemies, block bullets and slice through metal. Iron Man has helped to make the shield almost indestructible.

Iron Man

Tony Stark is heir to the Stark
Industries fortune and an expert
engineer. On a trip to Vietnam to
test weaponry, he was injured in an
explosion and captured by a local
warlord. A piece of shrapnel became
lodged close to his heart, so Stark built
the first Iron Man suit to protect his
heart and also help him escape.

He is now one of the most
important members of the
Avengers and often uses his
fortune to fund the team.

Iron Man's suit

His suit is powered by miniature
batteries built into the chest plate.
The boots contain air jets that help
him to fly.

Avengers headquarters

Every Super Hero team needs a secret base. The Stark family's mansion in New York served as the Avengers' first headquarters. The interior was adapted to suit their needs and Iron Man and Thor also pushed the building back from the street. Unfortunately, the mansion was destroyed in an explosion.

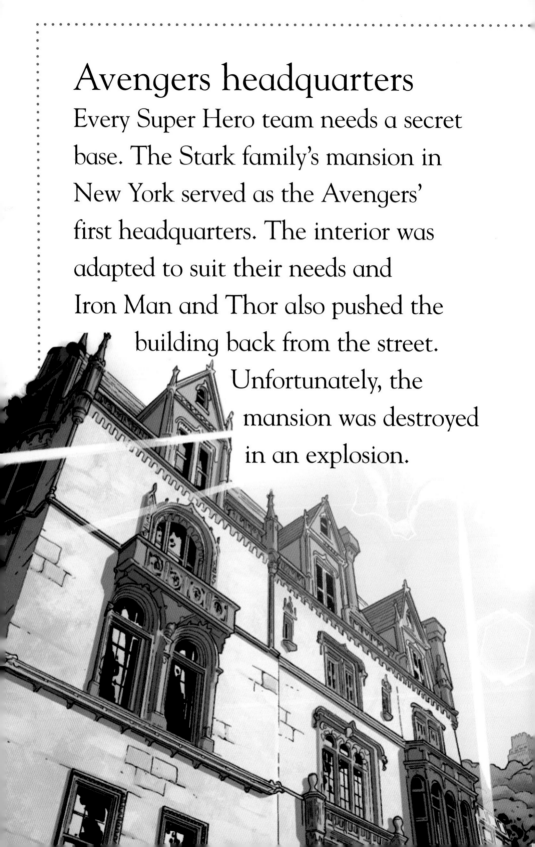

The Avengers now meet at Stark Tower, also owned by the Stark family. The tower has almost collapsed several times, once during a fierce battle between the Hulk and Iron Man.

Stark Tower is now called "Avengers Tower" by most people. It has 93 stories.

Jarvis

Edwin Jarvis was a loyal butler for the Stark family and now serves the Avengers. He often gets caught up in the team's adventures.

Super siblings

Mutant brother-sister duo, Scarlet Witch and Quicksilver, possess great super powers. Iron Man recruited them for Captain America's Avengers team. The team became known as "Cap's Kooky Quartet", with Hawkeye as the fourth member of the group.

Quicksilver is so speedy that he can run up walls, across water and even into the future! Captain America trained him in hand-to-hand combat so he is also an excellent fighter.

Scarlet Witch has mystical powers and can cast spells on her foes. She wears red and has a fierce temper. A mental breakdown caused her to fatally attack her team-mates and destroy the Avengers' Mansion.

Hawkeye

Hawkeye learned his skills with the bow and arrow while working in a circus and is now the best marksman Earth has ever seen. When he met Black Widow, she was a spy on a mission to destroy Iron Man. Hawkeye decided to help her, but later regretted this decision. So he changed sides and eventually joined the Avengers. Now Hawkeye uses his skills to fight Super Villains rather than Super Heroes!

Skycycle
Hawkeye travels around on a Skycycle, which looks like a snowmobile. It is voice-activated and has hands-free steering letting him aim while riding it.

Black Widow

Natasha Romanova was born in Russia. When she was young, she was a talented ballerina.

Natasha later became a top spy and her code name was Black Widow. She was trained by the terrorist group HYDRA and was once sent on a mission to spy on Tony Stark.

The Super Hero Hawkeye inspired Black Widow to leave HYDRA and work with the intelligence agency SHIELD and the Avengers instead. She is famous for her terrifying "widow's bite" – a bracelet-like gadget that fires electric bolts at her enemies.

Super pair
Hawkeye saved Black Widow's life during a battle with Iron Man. This led to a Super Hero romance.

Wolverine

Wolverine is more than 100 years old, but his incredible mutant ability to heal makes him almost indestructible. He first helped the Avengers during a battle in the ancient Savage Land and later became an official member of the team. Wolverine also has a long history with the X-Men mutant Super Hero team. Although he is not a team player by nature, Wolverine is a powerful and loyal member of both teams.

Adamantium
Wolverine's skeleton is made from Adamantium, which is the strongest metal on Earth. He also has razor-sharp, retractable claws.

United front

The Avengers is not the only team of Super Heroes around. Other Super Heroes also prefer to work together to defeat the most troublesome Super Villains. The Avengers have fought on the same side as many other groups such as the X-Men and the Fantastic Four.

Several Avengers have been members of other Super Hero teams over the years. Quicksilver joined X-Men and Captain America has often fought alongside the Fanstastic Four.

Fantastic Four consists of the Invisible Woman, the Thing, Human Torch and Mr. Fantastic, who also heads the team.

X-Men is a mutant Super Hero team led by Professor X. Other X-Men include Colossus, Wolverine, Cyclops and Storm.

31

Other Avengers

Over the years, there have been several different Avengers teams. Some are offshoots, others are copycats while some exist on alternate realities!

The Secret Avengers was formed to resist a new government rule of all Super Heroes registering and working for the government.

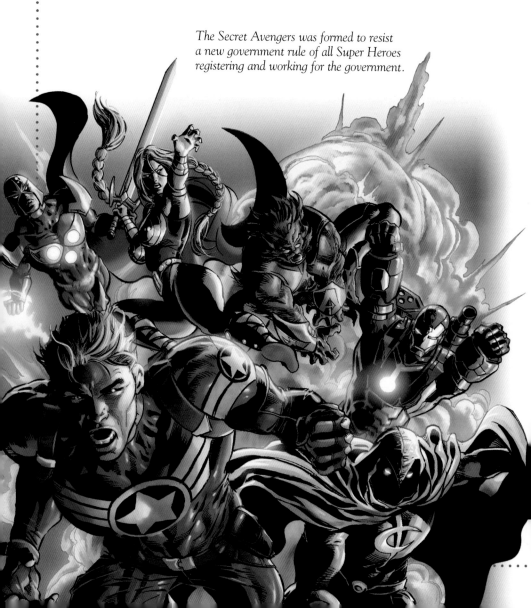

At one time, a group of aliens pretended to be the Avengers to wage a secret war and take over Earth.

The Secret Avengers was formed by Captain America and included Ant-Man and Black Widow. It was an undercover team that worked alongside the regular Avengers team.

The Young Avengers are teenagers with super powers, who model themselves on different Avengers heroes. The team was brought together by Iron Lad, who is a fan of Iron Man. They fought their first battle alongside Cap and Iron Man.

The Young Avengers once had to save Iron Lad from his future self.

The heroic age

Many villains were jealous of the Avengers' success and wanted to destroy the team. Evil forces tried to create disharmony within the group, and for a while they succeeded – the Super Heroes disbanded! However, a long and terrible siege in Asgard, led by the Super Villain Norman Osborn, eventually brought the team together again.

A new age dawned – the age of the hero! Super Heroes were back in control. Thor, Cap and Iron Man banded a new Avengers team together and Earth finally began to feel safe once more.

Maria Hill

Maria Hill was a spy but then joined the law enforcement agency SHIELD as its director. She was not very popular with the Avengers during this time. However, she eventually gained their trust when she disobeyed the President and cancelled a bombing that could have seriously injured the Avengers. Soon afterwards, Cap chose her to lead the Avengers in the new heroic age. Although she has no super powers, Maria Hill is an expert martial artist and markswoman.

Leaders
Many Super Heroes have led the Avengers in its long history, including Hawkeye, the Wasp, Iron Man and Captain Marvel.

Spider-Man

Peter Parker was an ordinary teenager until a bite from a radioactive spider gave him super powers. He gained superhuman strength, speed and spider-like agility. Parker then built himself web-shooters that allow him to create strong webs and stick to any surface. Spider-Man was born! Parker also designed himself a suit and a mask to keep his identity a secret.

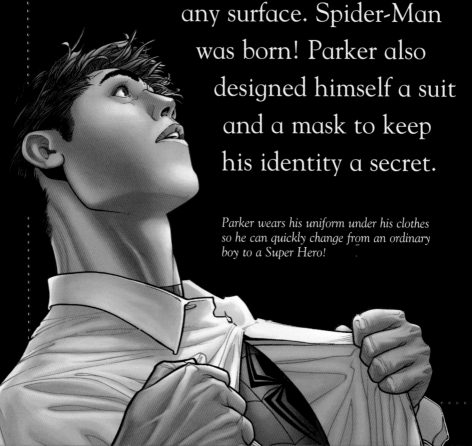

Parker wears his uniform under his clothes so he can quickly change from an ordinary boy to a Super Hero!

Spider-Man has fought alongside
the Avengers in many battles before
officially joining the team.

Spider-Woman

Spider-Woman started life as Jessica Drew. Her father Dr. Drew injected her with a spider serum in order to save her from radiation poisoning. The serum not only kept her alive, but it also gave her special spider powers.

An adhesive liquid secreted in her soles and palms allows Spider-Woman to stick to any surface.

Spider-Woman has superhuman strength, speed and reflexes, and can unleash venom blasts strong enough to kill. Like a spider, she can walk up walls using only her hands and feet. Spider-Woman was originally trained by the terrorist organisation HYDRA, but she left when she realised they were an evil organisation. She joined the intelligence agency SHIELD before becoming a member of the Avengers.

Captain Britain

Brian Braddock was a quiet, brainy boy until he was involved in a motorcycle accident. A legendary magician named Merlin appeared and transformed Braddock into Captain Britain – upholder of British laws and values. Captain Britain wears an amulet around his neck, which gives him super powers, including enhanced perception so he can detect mystical forces such as spells.

Captain Britain has teamed with Captain America many times to defeat common foes.

Captain Britain has battled
many Super Villains over time.
He is the newest recruit to join
the Avengers team.

Protector

Protector is also known as Noh-Varr. He is a Kree who ended up on Earth after his ship crashed. He is one of the most recent recruits on the Avengers team. The Kree are known for their size and strength, but Protector is even stronger than the average Kree. He can defy gravity and dodge bullets easily. He is a very skilled marksman and an excellent pilot.

Kree
The Kree are an alien race from the planet Hala. They are known for being very strong and tough, but they need special breathing apparatus when they are on Earth.

The future

They may have a roster of Super Heroes that is always changing and even some copycat teams, but one thing is certain – when the mighty Avengers are around, Earth is a safer place. Many Super Villains have tried to defeat them – and some have nearly succeeded – but with the cry "Avengers Assemble!" Thor, Captain America, Iron Man and the rest of the team won't hesitate to leap into action. The future will surely bring many new and dangerous adventures, but the Avengers are always ready!

Glossary

Alternate reality
A separate world
with the same Avengers
members, but where
they face different
adventures.

Avenge
To punish or hurt someone
for causing injury or doing
harm in general.

Code name
A secret name used
to identify someone.

Cybernetic
Something that
has the technology
to communicate with
and control animals and
living beings that do
not understand
human language.

Disharmony
When people are not
in agreement and there
is conflict and a lack
of harmony.

Enforcement
To make sure rules and
laws are obeyed.

Fatally
Resulting in death.

Gamma rays
Rays of electromagnetic
radiation.

Heir
One who inherits the
fortune and company of a
person on his or her death.

Humility
To have a modest
opinion about oneself
and not be boastful.

Indestructible
Something that
cannot be destroyed.

Lure
To trick someone into
doing something.

Marksman/markswoman
A man or a woman who
is an expert at shooting
at a target.

Mutant
Someone who has special
abilities due to changes
in their DNA or genes.

Mystical
Something that relates
to mind and spirit.

Offshoot
A branch of a bigger
organisation.

Patriotism
Loyalty towards
one's country.

Perception
The ability to see,
hear, or become aware
of something through
the senses.

Radiation
The discharge of energy
in the form of
electromagnetic waves.

Reflexes
The ability to act
automatically,
without thinking.

Retractable
Something that can be
pulled or drawn back in.

Roster
A list of members of
a team and their turns
of duty.

Serum
A liquid that is made
to ensure certain results.

Shrapnel
Fragments of a
bomb thrown out
in an explosion.

Siege
A planned attack to
capture a place by
surrounding it.

Stamina
The ability to be
physically active for
long periods of time.

Summon
To order someone to
be present somewhere.

Superhuman
Someone with
extraordinary strength
and powers.